KU-693-629

STEVE WRIGHT'S
FURTHER
FACTOIDS

STEVE WRIGHT'S FURTHER FACTOIDS

Steve Wright

with Jessica Rickson

HarperCollins*Publishers*

HarperCollins*Publishers*
77–85 Fulham Palace Road,
Hammersmith, London W6 8JB

www.harpercollins.co.uk

First published by HarperCollins*Entertainment* 2007
This edition published 2008
1

Copyright © Steve Wright 2007

Photographs © Getty Images 2007

The Author asserts the moral right to
be identified as the author of this work

A CIP catalogue record for this book
is available from the British Library

ISBN-13 978 0 00 725518 4

Printed and bound in Italy by
Legoprint S.p.A.

All rights reserved. No part of this publication may be
reproduced, stored in a retrieval system, or transmitted,
in any form or by any means, electronic, mechanical,
photocopying, recording or otherwise, without the prior
permission of the publishers.

ULTIMATE
FACTOIDS
FROM THE SHOW

A **'flexitarian'** describes 'a vegetarian who occasionally eats meat'.
Miles Mendoza

Every day in the UK a total of **£871 million** is in the nation's pockets.
Tim Smith

70 metres of **red carpet** is laid down every year for Britain's BAFTA Television Awards.
Janey Lee Grace

There are over 26 million separate **letterboxes** in Great Britain.
Old Woman

Nearly 40% of British students say they have stolen a traffic cone or shopping trolley on a night out... *It had to be a night out because they don't get up till lunchtime.*

Apparently, polar bear fur is not white. It's see-through but the light shines through the hairs to makes them look white against the bear's black skin... *P.S. Never let a polar bear mount a Fox's Glacier Mint.*

Insects outnumber humans one billion to one.

The number of people worldwide who speak French as a first or second language is 128 million... *And will they cooperate?*

At McDonald's in New Zealand, they serve **apricot** pies instead of apple ones.

Shrimps' hearts are in their heads...

And so is yours sometimes.

Only one person in two billion will live to be 116 or older...
And it's Jimmy Young.

A "funambulist" is a **tight-rope** walker.

Dubai has 17% of the world's cranes.

The average garden-variety caterpillar has **248** muscles in its head.

Bird flu aside, 426,000 Britons are allergic to birds... *(And don't they know it.)*

There are 35,000 hectares *(rhymes with Hannibal Lector)* of **peas** grown in the UK each year, equivalent to about 70,000 football pitches.

Despite the almost certainty of being shouted at and humiliated by **Sir Alan Sugar**, more than 20,000 hopefuls applied to be on this year's *The Apprentice*.

It has come to my attention that if you spend one hour walking along London's Oxford Street, you'll get jostled an average of **100 times**. *Also, I myself was pickpocketed outside Selfridges in Oxford Street, but thankfully the thief actually took my pocket, and left the wallet.*

No two **cornflakes** look the same. *You don't believe me? Then check yourself.*

People turn up to the set of the BBC daytime TV show *Doctors* and try to register at the Mill Health Centre, believing it to be a real surgery.

**Consecotaleophobia is having the fear of ...
chopsticks.** *(And spelling.)*

Ugly Betty **is not ugly,** *nor is she grotesque, rhymes with desk.*

Ahead of one of his restaurants opening, bucketmouth TV chef Gordon Ramsay had more than 4,200 Brits asking to dine there – even though it's in New York. He had enough calls to book it up for 2 years. *Even Donald Trump couldn't get a table.*

In a "Smells of Childhood" survey from this year, **nit shampoo** came first, followed by **Play-Doh**. *And third was your Gran who smelled largely of mints and old books.*

Now from my "Only in America" file: Arizona's "Heart Attack Grill" has introduced a new menu item, the "Quadruple Bypass Burger". It's stacked with four beef patties, cheese, onions, tomatoes and fried bacon. The **8,000 calorie** beast provides more than three times the intake a normal person needs each day. *I'll have two please, and statins for dessert.*

A London mum named her baby **John Lewis** after going into labour in the store in Brent Cross Shopping Centre. *Just as well he wasn't born in Virgin Megastore, or Tesco Metro.*

Are you aware that a **beer** called "Tail-wagger" with no alcohol has been brewed just for dogs by pet-shop owner Gerrie Berendson in Zelham, Holland?

Seven fifths of the population don't understand fractions!

In 2007, the new official shortest sentence in the English language is "I am." *The longest is "I do"...*

Tom Cruise and Katie Holmes's wedding kiss lasted **three minutes**. *After Tom climbed up on a box. Just kidding Tom, you know I love you. In fact I was only on a TV show the other day jumping up and down on a chair.*

This factoid from the archives of the *Plymouth Evening Herald*... In the sixties, Prime Minister Harold Wilson liked to travel to the Scilly Isles. This meant taking the train to Plymouth. One evening, when Harold is getting off the train, an old Devonshire newspaper seller on the platform shouts out in his Devonshire accent, "Evening Herald", to which the Prime Minister replies, "Good evening, my man."

10,000 residents in Juneau, Alaska, lost electricity after a bald eagle lugging a deer head crashed into a power transmission system. *Cries of oh deer!*

Socialite, party animal and ex jail bird **Paris Hilton** wears a size 11 shoe. Many top designers don't make

their shoes in an 11, so they have them custom made just for her.

Meanwhile, top chef **Gordon F Ramsay** takes a size 15 shoe!

Grease is the Word judge **David Gest** is an avid collector of Hollywood memorabilia and his collection of items belonging to ex-wife Liza Minnelli's mother, Judy Garland, is said to be the largest in the world.

Comedian **Jimmy Carr** has a pink orchid named after him.

Footballer **Wayne Rooney** proposed to his childhood sweetheart **Coleen McLoughlin** on the forecourt of a BP garage when she was 17 with a £25,000 diamond engagement ring. *And he was also lucky enough to get Tiger Tokens, a free Coca-Cola glass and a fold-down deckchair.*

During the World Cup 2006, **Coleen McLoughlin** made a 900-mile round trip from Germany to Liverpool – for a haircut.

Singer **Pete Doherty** achieved 11 grade As at GCSE – 5 of which were A-star.

Early in his career, movie star **Hugh Grant** was often credited as "Hughie Grant".

Madonna and fellow singer **Gwen Stefani** are distant cousins. *No Doubt about that.*

The word "factoid" was given **7 points** on the TV show *Countdown* in 2006.

Did you know that "**dilogy**" is a term used in Hollywood to describe an original movie and its sequel? Three linked movies are a trilogy. Two movies – such as *Bridget Jones' Diary* and *Bridget Jones: The Edge of Reason* – are a dilogy. *But "dilogy" is such a naff word that it's never used publicly.*

Mile for mile, the **Isle of Wight** is the most haunted island in the world. *Don't tell Derek Acorah or Living TV, they'll be all over it.*

Can this next factoid really be true? You decide... The French word for **paperclip** is "trombone".

Victoria Beckham's mum Jackie Adams **STILL** keeps every single press cutting which mentions her daughter... *She must be living in a warehouse by now then, in LA of course.*

The chicken came first.

Truro beekeeper Richard Harrison did not know why he kept being stung – until an expert said the bees hated his new shower gel. *And they didn't like his hair either. And those hideous shirts have to go. And another thing... silly socks.*

According to British Law, while it's an **offence** to drop litter on the pavement, unbelievably it's not an offence to throw it over someone's garden wall. *Well, that explains a lot. I'm going to have to talk to those dustmen.*

An average record shop needs to sell at least two copies of a CD per year to make it worth stocking, according to *Wired* magazine.

"Ah non, le quantum physics ce ne pas difficile!"

Movie star Nicole Kidman is **scared** of butterflies. "I jump out of planes, I could be covered in cockroaches, I do all sorts of things, but I just don't like the feel of butterflies' bodies," she says.

Baboons are so clever that they can tell the difference between English and French. Zookeepers at Port Lympne Wild Animal Park in Kent are having to learn French to communicate with the baboons, which had been transferred from a Paris zoo... *Whatever next – their own reality TV show?*

One in 10 Scandinavians is allegedly conceived in an Ikea bed.

The London borough of Westminster has an average of 20 pieces of chewing gum for every square metre of pavement. *And did you know that chewing gum can only be removed with*

CILIT BANG?!

Bosses at Madame Tussauds spent **£10,000** separating the models of Brad Pitt and Jennifer Aniston when they split up. It was the first time the museum had two people's waxworks joined together. *It's a peculiar thing but the last time I went to Madame Tussauds the manager said, "Could you keep moving, Mr Wright, we're stocktaking."*

At the time of writing, Her Majesty The Queen has never operated a **computer**. This she told Bill Gates as she awarded him an honorary knighthood.

One in four people in the UK still don't know 192, the old number for directory enquiries, has in fact been abolished.

A **Welshman** has had a slice of ham and pineapple pizza tattooed on the back of his head. It took three hours to complete and features three types of ham, chunks of pineapple and strands of cheese dripping down his neck.

A **Chinese man** recently married *himself* to express his "dissatisfaction with reality". The 39 year old, from Zhuhai city, married a life-sized foam cut-out of himself wearing a woman's bridal dress.

A **sci-fi fan** has spent 30 years and £30,000 building his own flying saucer. The builder put the machine together in his garage in Michigan in the USA, using aviation books.

A **graffiti artist** recreated the ceiling of the Sistine Chapel in a run-down building in Iowa. The man and his family spent their life savings, and his parents have taken out a second mortgage, to pay for the project.

An eccentric known as **The Mole Man** was banned from his home after digging a 60-foot network of tunnels beneath it. The 75 year old spent 40 years burrowing under his 20-room house, removing 100 cubic metres of earth with a spade and pulleys.

A **Turkish student** hoping to get into the record books gave the wrong answers to every question in a university entrance exam. The chap, from Ankara, deliberately answered all 180 questions wrong as a form of protest against the national university entrance examinations.

Two **motorists** who model themselves on the Blues Brothers were allowed to wear shades on their driving licence photos. Tribute singers Jake and Elwood talked DVLA bosses into bending the rules.

A **British millionaire** bought an entire Bulgarian coastal resort with a view to naming it after himself. He paid £3 million for the town and said locals are "quite excited" about it being renamed Alexander.

A **59-year-old man** who wanted to prove he was still as strong as a horse pulled a carriage 430 miles across Hungary. He started at Zahony on the country's eastern border, and dragged the 66-stone carriage to Szombathely on the western border in 22 days.

A **teenager** in India became famous for his ability to take in milk through his nose and to squirt it out of his eyes. He sucks milk up his nostrils and squirts it up to 12 feet through his tear ducts, and the feat has earned him a place in the *Limca Book of Records*, India's version of the *Guinness Book of World Records*.

A German man took legal action against the **Easter Bunny** for grievous bodily harm. The party pooper, from Berlin, filed a complaint with prosecutors, accusing the bunny of causing addiction to chocolate which leads to heart attacks, obesity and strokes.

A **Belgian student** sold the foreheads of himself and his friends to pay for his 20th birthday party. He put up their foreheads as advertising space as he had no money to buy food or drink for the bash. The online auction was won by a marketing firm in Waregem, which footed the bill for all party-goers to have the firm's logo painted on their foreheads for the night.

We British still buy the most compact discs in the world – an average of **3.2 per year**, compared to 2.8 in the USA and 2.1 in France. *Although as downloading becomes more prevalent these figures will no doubt go down. Factoids will keep you posted.*

The name **Lego**, as in the children's toy, comes from two Danish words "leg godt", meaning "play well". It also means "I put together" in Latin.

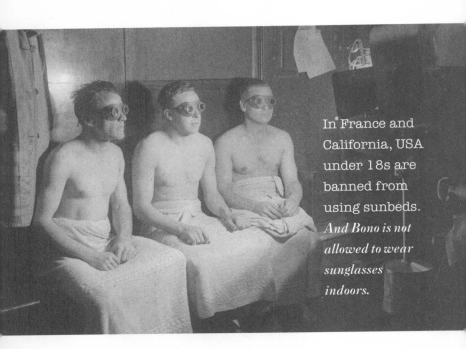

In France and California, USA under 18s are banned from using sunbeds. *And Bono is not allowed to wear sunglasses indoors.*

The average UK employee spends **14 working days** a year on personal e-mails, phone calls and web browsing.

Britain's smallest church, near Malmesbury, Wiltshire, holds just one service a year. It measures **4m by 3.6m** and has one pew. *Tom Cruise did consider it for a wedding venue. And Ronnie Corbett's a regular.*

Only **36%** of the world's newspapers are tabloid.

The word **"trivia"** comes from the Latin "tri + via", meaning three streets. In ancient Rome an information booth was situated where three streets met. *And Romans of course invented the light switch, nuclear weapons, hair, throats, books, heating, Italy, carburettors, curling tongs, the London Underground, Geiger Counters, Venus, Specsavers, Troy Tempest from Stingray, feet, Ken Livingstone and hot springs. And baldness, Richard Madeley's chest hair, BBC4, the steam iron and the pony.*

Blockbusters legend **Bob Holness** used to present a game show called *Take A Letter. Bet it was a P please, Bob*.

Britain came **37th** in a list of best countries in which to live, judged on things like climate, culture, economy and freedom. Top country was France. *I demand a recount*.

Tom and Jerry made their debut as Jasper and Jinks in the 1940 film *Puss Gets The Boot*.

Half the people surveyed by the Samaritans said they're more stressed than five years ago, with **money** overtaking work as the top stress factor.

As well as protecting the heart and reducing the risk of cancer, a glass of red wine also helps slow the ageing process. *Give me a couple more then*.

The best music video ever was Duran Duran's "Rio", beating Michael and Janet Jackson's hit "Scream". *That's according to Simon Le Bon, though.*

A three-toed sloth spends 80 per cent of its time asleep. *Wake up, Sloth! You've only got three toes, Friend!*

The record for eating **38** hard-boiled eggs is **1 minute 15 seconds**.

The *Mahabharata* is the longest poem in the world, with more than **74,000** verses and needing 18 large volumes to print it.

The longest ever ski jump was 239 metres.

Scientists have located a sort of **bottleneck** of nerves in the brain which explains why we find it hard to do two things at once. *Well, us blokes do anyway.*

Actress **Billie Piper's** parents changed her given name from Lianne three weeks after registering her birth, after they decided they liked the name Billie more.

The Queen star **Dame Helen Mirren** was born Ilyena Vasilievna Mironov. Her father was of Russian origin.

X Factor star and *Britain's Got Talent* judge **Simon Cowell** says that the first time he gave a criticism was at age four when he looked at his mother's white fuzzy pillbox hat and remarked, "Mum, you look like a poodle."

Doctor Who star **David Tennant** has auditioned for Scottish police drama *Taggart* 16 times – but has never been given a part.

As a toddler, movie actress **Penelope Cruz** would re-enact TV commercials for her family's amusement.

Actor **Leonardo DiCaprio's**
middle name is Wilhelm.

Comic Relief Does Fame Academy winner **Tara Palmer-Tomkinson** is a trained concert pianist, and practises for 90 minutes every day. *There must be a piano in Harvey Nicks, then.*

According to reports, movie star and singer Jennifer Lopez can't be expected to stoop and tie her shoe lace, so she employs an official "shoe fastener" instead.

Courtney Cox is the only member of the TV show *Friends* cast not to receive an Emmy nomination for her work on the show.

Celebrity Big Brother winner **Chantelle** originally applied to be in Big Brother 6. However, after some encouragement from PR guru Max Clifford, the show's producers put her in the *Celebrity Big Brother* house instead.

Women say an average 20,000 words a day compared to men's 7,000. *I don't want to talk about it.*

Ozzy Osbourne, in a job that would come back to haunt him in later life, was once a **labourer** in a slaughterhouse.

The avocado has the most calories of any fruit.

The actress Jill Halfpenny began her TV acting career on *Byker Grove. She was Jill Farthing back then.*

If each of the UK's ten million office workers used one less staple a day, **120 tonnes** of steel would be saved every year.

Sixty per cent of all journeys made by Dutch people over the age of 69 are by bike.

Australia's victory over England in The Ashes in **2006** was the first whitewash since 1921. *The Wizards of Oz*.

A woman who won **£688,260** with a £2 accumulator flutter on the horses picked the winners with birth dates.

From *EastEnders*, the name Walford is a mix of Walthamstow and Stratford.

Council bosses in Swindon, Wiltshire, have responded to huge public demand by publishing a picture **postcard** of a roundabout near the town. The so-called Magic Roundabout already has t-shirts and keyrings dedicated to it.

The top best-selling book of all time is the Bible, which has been printed in more than **2,000** languages and has sold over six billion copies. *Not been mentioned in Richard and Judy's Book Club yet, though.*

A record number of women over 40 became pregnant last year... **Russell Brand says he wasn't responsible. He was away in Los Angeles.**

According to the World Health Organisation, there are approximately **100 million** acts of sexual intercourse each day. *Way too much information!*

The children's television show **Tiswas** stood for Today is Saturday, Wear a Smile.

"Cabbaged" and "fabaceae" are the longest words that can be played on a musical instrument.

And fickleheaded **and** fiddledeedee are the longest words consisting only of letters in the first half of the alphabet.

Movie star Kate Winslet and "olde tyme" comedian Norman Wisdom have something in common – they've both appeared in the TV show *Casualty*.

The New Zealand basketball team are known as **The Tall Blacks.**

The first female to circumnavigate *(sounds painful)* the globe was Krystyna Choynowska-Liskiewicz. *That's easy for you to say.*

TV star Oprah Winfrey's parents wanted to use the biblical name **Orpah**, but the midwife couldn't spell so it became Oprah.

A survey of the quietest town in Britain found Torquay is **100 times** less noisy than Newcastle upon Tyne.

We produce enough waste in **two hours** to fill London's Albert Hall. *But why should we want to do that? Wouldn't it get in Eric Clapton's way?*

Eighty-two per cent of speeding offences are committed by a man. *And he should stop it immediately.*

Liverpool player Peter Crouch wore a shirt with 12 on the back and 21 on the front in England's football friendly with Uruguay.
Because Peter is wacky.

Dramatic changes in our **climate** mean we could lose the four seasons. *And they were a damn good group. "Big Girls Don't Cry"*…

Lacrosse is the fastest growing sport in the USA. *Apart from eating.*

The final episode of *M*A*S*H* attracted a record TV audience of more than **109 million**.

The Test cricketer of the 20th century, according to a panel of 100 cricketers and experts, was Sir Donald Bradman.

The hit "Wooden Heart" is adapted from the German folk song "Muss I Denn". *We'll have to ask Elvis about that. Thangu vey much.*

A kitten called Georgia that escaped from her carrier on a New York subway platform was rescued by track workers after 25 days in the underground tunnels. *Georgia on my mind…*

Disgraced President **Richard Nixon** was so worried about his grades at Law School that he broke into his Dean's office to find his results. He discovered he was top of the class.

Winston Churchill's family motto was "Fiel Pero Desdichado", meaning "Faithful But Unfortunate".

Notorious villain **Attila the Hun** died of a nosebleed on his wedding night because he was too drunk to notice his nose was bleeding.

Some Argentine fans are so in awe of "Hand of God" football villain **Diego Maradona** they worship him as a god, with their own "Maradonian" religion. This involves following "ten commandments" – one of which is to call your son Diego.

Russian dictator **Joseph Stalin's** face was left badly scarred by smallpox, which he suffered from as a child. He later had photographs retouched to make his pockmarks less noticeable.

Muhammad Ali learned to box after his bike was stolen while he and a friend were at the Columbia Auditorium. The then young Cassius Clay found a policeman in a gym and told him he was going to "whup" whoever stole his bike. The policeman told him, "You better learn to box first." So he did, and the rest is history.

A recent survey voted **Jack the Ripper** the worst Briton of the last 1,000 years.

Serial killer **Charles Manson** recorded an album called *Lie* in an effort to spread his beliefs.

Rowing hero **Steve Redgrave** won an Olympic Gold medal by a margin of just 0.38 seconds.

Although known during his life, and in history, as a tyrant, before his death **Ivan the Terrible** was actually re-christened as the monk Jonah and buried in his monk's habit.

Mother Theresa was born Agnes Bojaxhiu. After taking her first vows as a nun, she chose the name Theresa after the patron saint of missionaries.

Adolf Hitler left school with no qualifications.

Gangster **Al Capone** was the only real person to appear as a character in *The Adventures of Tintin* series of comic books.

Superman's alter ego, **Clark Kent**, was named after American actors Clark Gable and Kent Taylor.

The name of James Bond villain **Blofeld** was inspired by the English cricket commentator Henry Blofeld's father, with whom Bond creator Ian Fleming went to school. *Look out, he's got a dangerous cat, but he's out for a duck.*

Meanwhile, James Bond himself was named after an American ornithologist, a Caribbean bird expert who was the author of the definitive guide book *Birds of the West Indies*.

The flashing lights on the original *Doctor Who* Daleks were indicator lights from an old Morris 1100.

The person who does the housework at home walks an average of **7,000 miles** in their lifetime doing the vacuuming. *Sucking blowing blowing sucking blowing blowing sucking sucking blowing sucking...*

Ikea gave all its **9,000** staff a bicycle as its contribution to tackling global warming. Bet they were worried when they got letters telling them to get on their bikes.

"Rugged" is a two-syllable word that can be made *one* syllable by adding letters to it to make the word "shrugged".

Women blink nearly twice as much as men.
Why...?

Harry Randall is Cockney rhyming slang for **candle**. *Fair enough, but who's Harry Randall?*

Renoir had to paint with the brush tied to his fingers because of rheumatism.

Drinking three cups of coffee a day can cut the risk of developing Alzheimer's disease.

Louis XIII *(that's 13th in real money)* appointed a Royal Anagrammist (*bloke what does anagrams*) for a salary of **£1,200** a year.

Pensioners now prefer surfing the net to traditional old people's pastimes of gardening, DIY and walking. *And eating boiled sweets.*

The "Mona Lisa" has no eyebrows – it was the fashion in Renaissance Florence to shave them off. *She's also got a tat of a spider on her neck if you look closely, and her tongue is pierced, which accounts for the painful smile.*

Postmen and women **walk** further than secretaries in their work, a global study found.

The average number of sexual partners a man has during his life is **14.56**. *Must have been interrupted during the 15th...*

Sack races were banned at a community's annual festival because the cost of insuring against injury became too high. Out went the three-legged race and egg-and-spoon at the "fun day" in **Hartlepool**. *Eggs can break easily when dropped, that's a fact.*

Psychologists at Aberdeen University reckon the best way to woo a woman is to chat up her mate.

Fathers tend to determine the height of their child, mothers their weight. *Hmm, I think I'll make him 6 foot 2.*

Fulham's Moritz Volz scored the **15,000th** goal in Premiership history in the last game of last year. *15,000 Volz...*

According to a poll in the *British Medical Journal*, the most significant health breakthrough of all time was not antibiotics, vaccines or anaesthetic but... sanitation.

Scientists have found the brain has a kind of screensaver that automatically kicks in when we're idle, allowing our mind to wander or daydream.

Parents spend 3,000 more hours of quality time with their first-born child than with subsequent children – and first-borns perform better at school and earn more money in later life, according to researchers. *Mind you, the researchers were all second-born kids, so what do they know?*

A half-eaten banana signed by *GMTV* presenter **Kate Garraway** fetched £1,650 on an auction website.

Before becoming a professional dancer, *Strictly Come Dancing* star **Brendan Cole** worked as a builder.

Dragons' Den star and multi-millionaire Duncan Bannatyne began his business career as an ice-cream man, after buying an ice-cream van for 450 quid.

Comedian **Russell Brand** has been arrested 11 times, once for stripping off at an anti-globalisation protest.

Desperate Housewives star **Eva Longoria** is the only one among her parents' children to have dark skin, dark eyes and dark hair. Her three sisters all have fair hair, blue eyes and pale skin. Eva thought for a long time that she was adopted because she looked so different.

In the mid 90s, a photo of fellow Desperate Housewife **Teri Hatcher**, wrapped in nothing but a red Superman cape, became the most downloaded image on America Online.

Jennifer Aniston, Kate Moss and **Kelly Osbourne** all have heart tattoos, whilst **Sienna Miller, Britney Spears, Victoria Beckham** and **Lindsay Lohan** all have stars.

Borat star **Sacha Baron Cohen** went to the same school as Matt Lucas of *Little Britain*, and funnyman David Baddiel.

All **emperor penguins** with film careers have *Happy Feet*.

Beatrix Potter left the National Trust **4,000 acres** in the Lake District to be preserved for the nation.

Judge John Deed (*not a real judge*) actor Martin Shaw, once worked for a chemical company before being accepted at drama school.

Kisses given under the mistletoe are called loran-thaceous. *Am I bovvered?*

The funniest *Two Ronnies* sketch, according to the late Ronnie Barker, was the *Mastermind* take-off when the subject was answering the question before last. *No! I AIN'T BOVVERED!!*

The club with the longest name in the Football League is **Wolverhampton Wanderers**. *Which just beats The Used To Be Not Very Good Accrington Stanley.*

...and the only football team you can't colour in is Hull City. *Go on, try it.*

Parents in the USA have launched a **Birthdays Without Pressure** campaign to end the idea of providing bigger, better and more expensive parties than everyone else.

The things they say: "It was really difficult for us, playing in the midday sun with that **three o'clock** kick-off." – David Beckham

The owner of a car that was wrecked by a falling tree in **80mph** gales in Worcester returned to find it had a (crushed) parking ticket on the smashed windscreen.

The artist George Stubbs used to suspend dead horses from the ceiling so he could draw them while they weren't moving. *That makes Damien Hirst seem normal.*

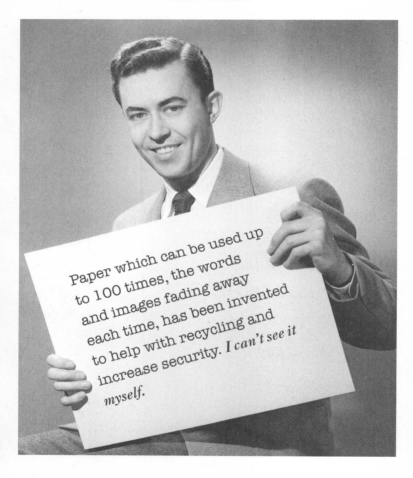

Paper which can be used up to 100 times, the words and images fading away each time, has been invented to help with recycling and increase security. *I can't see it myself.*

The only eight-letter word with four **Gs** in it is giggling. *You're having a laugh aren't you?*

The world's largest **lake** is Superior. *Well, that's an opinion.*

Health-conscious families are turning from wheat to **oats** at breakfast time, said *The Grocer* magazine, with sales of porridge rising by more than five per cent. *That's what you call oat cuisine. And if you can think of a better punch line than that, cross that out and put your own in!*

Swallows can't be bothered to fly south for winter migration any more because there are enough insects for them to feed on here. *And most of them have been to Brighton anyway.*

Researchers say the average woman puts on more than 15 stone during her life and then diets it off again.

Fifty-four minutes of an average working day is spent surfing the net. *And the other six minutes trying to load RealPlayer.*

A man fell **16 floors** from a hotel window in Minneapolis and survived when he landed in an awning just above the street.

 **Forty-six per cent** of the world has the blood group "O".

Lacy underwear with a luxury French label was draped around the Wiltshire village of Pouton for months on end. *Police are still examining the evidence...*

A couple who were married **60 years ago** had a celebration party in Sussex this year, and were joined by their best man – now aged 83 – and 78- and 80-year-old bridesmaids... *Unfortunately, the wedding cake had gone off and the best man forgot his speech – and teeth – twice!*

Shane Warne became the first man to take **700 Test wickets** when he bowled Andrew Strauss during the fourth Ashes Test in the winter of 2006.

Coronation Street was originally going to be called Florizel Street until the **tea lady** said it sounded like a disinfectant. *It's little known that their first choice was Dettol Avenue. Second choice –* *CLOSE, with BARRY SCOTT.*

CILIT BANG

Oasis frontman Noel Gallagher is said to have cried when he heard Manchester City fans singing "Wonderwall". *Was it that bad?*

A **French tourism** report shows its own citizens are among the rudest in the world, and a third of French people refuse to hold a conversation in English even when they know how to.

Recreational walking is the nation's favourite keep-fit pastime, ahead of swimming and going to the gym.

The title of the 70s TV programme The Old Grey Whistle Test *comes from the old maxim: "When the grey-haired doorman whistles your tune, you've got a hit on your hands."*

Australians once believed boiled onions cured worms in children; onions boiled or roasted cured a cold; and raw onions purified the blood... *Not as much as a burger, says Wrighty.*

The **juice of boiled nettles** is reported to be excellent for easing sciatica.

Eating **peanut butter** cures headaches, supposedly. *Unless you have a nut allergy. I myself am not allergic to nuts, just nutters.*

24 hours of eating **garlic soup** gets rid of a cough, it's said.

And here's some unusual ailments you wouldn't want to have...

ALICE IN WONDERLAND SYNDROME

Also called **micropsia**, people's visual perception is distorted so that objects which are close appear disproportionately tiny, as though viewed through the wrong end of a telescope. It owes its name to Lewis Carroll's Alice, who perceived things as too small or too big after taking magical medicines... *So a kind of tunnel vision. See "politicians".*

PICA

This is a compulsive **appetite for non-edible items**. People with PICA (rhymes with Mika) regularly eat **clay**, **stones**, **cigarette ash**, **paint**, **glue**, **laundry starch**, **ice** and even their **own hair**. *One person I know*

who has this condition is Tim Smith, co-host on my Afternoon Show. In fact, he's eaten most of his hair completely off. And by the way kids – don't eat glue, you could come to a sticky end. And drinking paint won't give you a lovely finish.

FOREIGN ACCENT SYNDROME

Imagine suddenly putting on a totally convincing French accent. Or a brilliant Scottish lilt. Or perfect ice-cream Italian. Without warning, people can start speaking their **native tongue** with a **different accent**, which could sound anything from Swedish to South African.

ALIEN HAND SYNDROME

This bizarre syndrome involves totally **losing control of one hand**, which will do anything from gesticulating to unbuttoning clothes its owner is trying to put on with his or her other hand. The condition is also called **Dr Strangelove Syndrome**, thanks to Peter Sellers' inspired performance as Dr Strangelove in Stanley Kubrick's 1964 hit movie.

CAPGRAS SYNDROME

This involves the delusion that a significant other, such as a parent, spouse or other relative, has been **replaced by an imposter**.

HYPERTRICHOSIS

People with hypertrichosis have **hair growing all over the body** – including eyelids and even ears, which can sprout long curls. Some cases also have a little hairy appendage called a faun tail.

A woman from Worcester found a pearl in oysters she bought at Tesco (*rhymes with al fresco*). It was valued at £30 and Tesco said the chances of finding one were a million to one. *But if it goes well they'll do them as a Buy One Get One Free, with 100 extra Club Card points.*

Welsh movie star **Catherine Zeta Jones** first caught the eye of her future husband Michael Douglas with her appearance in the film *The Mask of Zorro*. *It must have fallen out when he was tying his shoelaces.*

You should keep your toothbrush at least six feet away from the toilet to avoid airborne particles resulting from the flush. *Or you could put the lid down.*

Earlier this year **Mark Beaumont** became the fastest person to cycle round the world, covering the **18,000 miles** in **195 days** (an average of nearly **100 miles** a day, since you ask).

Rudyard Kipling invented the game of snow golf, painting his balls red so they could be seen in the snow. *No funny comment required.*

Both legendary singer Rod Stewart and TV star Bradley Walsh played football for *Brentford* youth teams.

Health and safety officers refused permission for a Guy Fawkes bonfire at Ilfracombe Rugby Club, so they erected a big screen and projected dancing flames onto it.

The market for trousers with a waistband of **37 inches** or more is increasing by 15 per cent a year. *Somebody should tell Top Shop.*

Police dressed up as Santa's **elves** in Florida to act as decoys in trapping speeding drivers. *An elf and safety check, then…*

Batman was the first film in the UK to be given the new **12** rating.

The highest ever speed on skis was 156mph recorded last year by Italian Simone Origone. *He's still missing, or possibly still up in the air.*

Youngsters who skip breakfast are more likely to put on weight in adulthood as they make up for it later in the day by eating junk food.

The dial tone of a traditional telephone is in the key **F**.

More than three-quarters of a million **gifts** are ordered online at Amazon in a single day leading up to Christmas.

Sports psychologists at Exeter University say a happy home life improves your golf, because moral support is helpful to sportspeople.

The Loch Ness monster was voted the most famous **Scot** in a Britain-wide poll, beating Robert Burns, Sean Connery and Gordon Brown into the minor places. *So of course Nessie was the only monster to make the list.*

Children who spend **hours** playing online fantasy games can show the same signs of addiction as gamblers.

A possum travelled 12,000 miles in a crate of onions on a cargo ship from New Zealand before being found at Felixstowe, having lived on condensation and, well, onions.

There's a persistent myth that all the clocks in the movie *Pulp Fiction* are set to **4:20**. Although certainly all the clocks on the wall in the pawn shop are set to **4:20**, in the "Bonnie Situation", while Jimmy, Vince and Jules are drinking coffee in the kitchen, the clock clearly reads 8:15. And, when Vince and Jules go to retrieve the briefcase, it is "**7:22** in the a.m." *And by the way, do you know what they call a cheeseburger in Paris, France?*

For every 1% of broadband growth, newspaper circulation drops 0.2%.

 A driverless robotic **car** with an electronic brain and laser "eyes" that see everywhere at once has been built at Stanford University, California.

Tourists Gary Easton, and wife Maureen, arrived at their holiday cottage near **Bude**, Cornwall to find their toilet had been stolen. *People just nick anything these days. It's crap isn't it?*

HRH Prince Charles and Camilla spent Valentine's Day 2007 watching the Monty Python stage show *Spamalot* in London.

Scoleciphobia is the fear of worms. *They don't look scary to me, unless they get in your shepherd's pie.*

Shakespeare walked with a limp because of a congenital disability, it's recently been discovered. *But he also used to buy pants that were way too small.*

James Bond's favourite order of "vodka martini, shaken not stirred" was first uttered by Sean Connery in *Dr No* in **1962**.

The **giant panda** has been enjoying a mini baby boom after a record 30 babies were bred in captivity in 2006, bringing the total to 217.

When Radio 2's **Dermot O'Leary** told his dad he wanted to work in TV, his dad told him "no one makes any money out of telly, get a proper job". In 2007 Dermot signed a reported million-pound contract to present *X Factor*.

Doctor Who and *Torchwood* star **John Barrowman** got down to the last three for the title role of Will in American comedy *Will and Grace*, but was rejected on the grounds that he was "not gay enough". Barrowman is himself gay.

Brad Pitt turned down the role of an astronaut in *Apollo 13* to take his role in *Se7en*

In 2007, singer **Peter André** was rushed to Kingston General Hospital in Jamaica suffering from banana poisoning. He was reported to have eaten 50 bananas the previous day and was suffering from an extreme potassium overdose.

Prince Philip protested that comedienne **Catherine Tate** had gone too far during the Royal Variety Show when her "bovvered" character Lauren commented that "the old fella next to the Queen" appeared to be asleep.

Supermodel **Kate Moss** is reported to smoke 80 cigarettes a day.

TV host **Graham Norton** was the victim of a serious knife attack when he was in his 20s. He lost half the blood in his body and one lung collapsed.

Before making it into the group, Girls Aloud member **Nadine Coyle** had been a winner on the Irish version of the show, but had been disqualified when it was discovered that she had lied about her age and was too young to audition for the programme.

The British store Marks and Spencer's first ready-prepared meal was the Chicken Kiev in the late **70s**. *Back in the day it was called Chicken Kev, because it was mainly Kev who bought it.*

The International Tennis Federation stipulates that a tennis ball dropped onto concrete from 100 inches should bounce MORE than 53 inches and LESS than 58 inches. *Do they have to be playing tennis, or is that just generally? New balls please.*

After the release of the film *The Full Monty*, the Oxford English Dictionary's online edition had to be revised – the definition of the phrase "full monty" was expanded to take in its usage as a reference to total nudity.

The average mother spends **13 whole days** preparing for Christmas. And after all that, the average Christmas dinner lasts little more than two hours. *Unless you have seconds and thirds. We always*  *play Scrabble and then come back to it. Then it's turkey sandwiches for three weeks – that's what I used to think "cold turkey" was.*

Saffron – *who used to be the sixth Spice Girl* – is known as the king of spices; and it's actually the world's most expensive food by weight – it takes **120,000 crocus flowers**, *each picked by hand by Dale Winton*, to produce one kilogramme of saffron.

Strictly Come Dancing **presenter Tess Daly got her first showbiz break while still a teenager, appearing in two Duran Duran videos in 1990.**

The Usual Suspects movie star Gabriel Byrne's previous jobs included an archaeologist, a Gaelic and Spanish teacher, a cook, a toy-factory worker and a bullfighter. It wasn't until he was **29** that he discovered acting.

More than a **third** of Britain's cats and dogs – six million pets – are overweight. Eight in ten vets now run special clinics for overweight animals. *You should see the 30-stone poodle that eats five steaks a day, and four bowls of Viennetta.*

Following his 300mph car crash, *Top Gear*'s Richard Hammond developed a craving for **celery**. He previously wouldn't eat it.

TV show *Pinky and Perky* **was banned by the BBC in 1966 for being too political.** *You'd think they'd be more astounded that pigs could talk.*

Doctor Who **star David Tennant was born David MacDonald. He chose the surname Tennant after reading an interview with Neil Tennant of the Pet Shop Boys, shortly after being told he needed to change it to join the actors' union Equity.**

The quagga was a type of **zebra** which was hunted to extinction in the 19th century.

Most famously suffered by Eric Bristow in the 90s, the technical name for the condition endured by darts players when, for reasons unknown, they find they simply can't let go of the dart is **DARTITIS**. *Another condition they suffer from is ROTUNDITY.*

Almost **40 per cent** of women who work full-time are paid more than their husband or live-in boyfriend.

Sixties TV Western series *Bonanza* took its title from a word of Spanish origin used for a mine or vein rich in ore. *Isn't that fascinating? I'm in ore of that factoid.*

The Queen's granddaughter, Zara Phillips, became the first senior member of the Royal Family to receive an award in the honours system. She received an **MBE** for services to equestrianism in 2006.

The first Dickens TV adaptation was *A Christmas Carol* in 1943, starring William Podmore. At 60 minutes, it was then the longest TV play ever broadcast.

Three models were sent home from a fashion show in Madrid this year for being too **thin**. *Adios skellingtons!*

The reason *Big Brother*'s Jade Goody gave for not being able to finish the 2006 London Marathon? She had no idea what a mile was… *That's good enough for me.*

Harry Potter's middle name is James. *Round glasses.*

In 2006, all of the following were banned – paper planes at a Tunbridge Wells school, the word "prisoner" when referring to young offenders, and doormats because they pose a trip hazard, according to Bristol City Council.

James Bond was beaten at the US box office by a **dancing penguin** – *Casino Royale* took £21.5 million in its first weekend, while the animated tale *Happy Feet* grossed £22.4 million. *Penguin suit versus penguin.*

The greatest Cliff Richard song **EVER** was named as
"Miss You Nights" in a recent poll of BBC Radio 2 listeners.

In **2006** the total amount of digital information
sent in the form of email, blogs, mobile calls, photos
and TV would have filled 161 billion iPod Shuffles.
Rhymes with ruffles.

In 2006, **17%** of politicians around the world were female,
the highest number ever, and a rise of 9% in a decade.

Half the drivers surveyed
admitted experiencing **road rage**,
and it's reckoned more than a
million of us lose our temper
daily.

Deal Or No Deal's Noel Edmonds was once President of the Association of **Gateaux Hurlers**. *He wants to have his cake and eat it, that boy.*

Dale Winton regularly received the cane whilst at boarding school for **talking** after lights out.

Opportunity Knocks host Hughie Green once hosted a show in the then USSR. Cash prizes were forbidden, so the top prize was a television.

Catchphrase stalwart Roy Walker was once the Northern Ireland hammer throwing champion.

Anne Robinson developed her trademark wink during her time as presenter of *Points of View*. The director told her not to **wink**, so she insisted on winking at the end of every programme in defiance from then on.

The manufacturers of an Eamonn Holmes-endorsed DVD game about spelling had to reprint **10,000 copies** after his name was spelt incorrectly on the packaging.

It's A Knockout star Stuart Hall claims that he coined the footballing phrase "the beautiful game".

GMTV's Keith Chegwin appeared on the **1975 hit** "The Bump" by Kenny.

Ready Steady Cook's Ainsley Harriott was once a ball boy at Wimbledon.

Television legend **Sir David Frost** began his career as a reporter for a local television news programme. His bosses weren't impressed by his efforts, however, and believing that he didn't have a future in regional

broadcasting, refused to renew his contract.

Top Gear presenter Richard Hammond used to work as a "chicken chaser" at his local farm.

When **Ant and Dec** first met on the set of *Byker Grove* they didn't like each other. Even they didn't know who was who...

Jimmy Tarbuck turned down the chance to host *The Generation Game*.

Bob Monkhouse used to write **jokes** for many visiting American comedians, including Bob Hope, when they wanted topical gags for their British tours.

Match of the Day's Gary Lineker won the Golden Boot Award for being top scorer at the **1986 World Cup** in Mexico. He is the only English player ever to have received this award.

Countdown's Des O'Connor has an orange face.

Crackerjack presenter Eamonn Andrews originally hosted Double or Drop as a touring show for adults. The prize money would be doubled at each question up to a maximum of one pound.

Leslie Crowther never wanted to use the phrase "Come on down", whilst presenting *The Price is Right*, because his wife had thought it sounded brash.

Noises at night – such as a partner's snoring or aircraft passing overhead – increase your blood pressure even though you're asleep.

There are 206 bones in the adult human body but more than **300** in children as some of the bones fuse together as kids grow.

The surname Wright means a maker or **builder**. *I've always been Wright. Sorry mate, I was on another job. That estimate I gave you has gone up. Didn't I tell you it's plus VAT? This is going to cost you, I'll have to go down Jewson and get the materials. We ran out of paint.*

Eating a bag of *watercress* is said to be a good cure for a hangover. *But don't eat the bag.*

There were **seven** white Christmases in the 20th century. The definition of a white Christmas is when at least one snowflake falls on the roof of the London Weather Centre. *That's nothing for Aled Jones to sing about.*

1.5 billion cups of tea are drunk throughout the world every day. *Mainly by me.*

Forty-six per cent of the world's water is in the Pacific Ocean.

Sir Stanley Matthews was the first footballer to be knighted. *Big shorts, too long.*

Butterflies **taste** with their feet. *Cheesy...*

A married couple is divorced in the UK every three minutes. *Even at quarter to four in the morning?*

Postmen in Victorian England were called **robins** because their uniforms were red. Christmas cards often showed a robin delivering them. That's also where we get the expression **"round robin"** from.

Sixty wives of the world's 100 richest men are **brunettes.**

Tantalus was a king in Greek mythology whose crimes were punished by having food and drink kept just out his reach. Hence the word **tantalise**. *Self-appointed gold star award factoid.*

Limelight was how a stage was lit before electricity was invented. Illumination was produced by heating blocks of lime until they glowed. Hence the expression **"in the limelight"**.

The ant can pull 30 times its own weight. *Whoops, there goes another rubber tree plant.*

Christmas cards were delivered on December 25 in the 19th century. *So much for progress.*

Women return to work an average 2.3 years after having a baby, compared to **6.7 years** 30 years ago.

"Plutoed" – to demote or devalue something, in honour of Pluto being kicked out of the Solar System for not being a full-time planet – was voted **Word of the Year in 2006.**

The only mention William Shakespeare ever made of his **wife** was in his last will and testament when he left her his "second best bed". *Wherefore art thou first best bed?*

More than half the people in the world have never made or received a telephone call.
*That ****er next to you on the train isn't one of them.*

Parents drive an average 1,664 miles – the distance from London to Istanbul – chauffeuring their children each year. *I'm not sure quite how many London kids go to school in Istanbul – that would be a hell of a school run.*

Gorillas sleep up to **fourteen hours** per day. *Lazy sods. Do not disturb, though.*

 In a standard pack of **playing cards** the queen holds flowers in her hands. *If you're going to San Francisco…*

Supermarkets have been criticised for selling **bottled water** at the equivalent of 57p a pint when beer was only 54p.

Christmas festivities were banned by **Oliver Cromwell** in 1647. Feasting and revelry on a holy day was considered immoral and anybody caught celebrating Christmas was arrested. *Or watching* It's A Wonderful Life.

Charitable donations made on credit and debit cards exceeded £1 **billion** for the first time in 2007; the average donation was **£44.75.**

Girls are better than boys at using **computers**, a study shows – but both sexes are better than their old mum and dad, who are sometimes a bit dipsy. *Go silver surfers!*

Losing the **Ashes** in Australia in the winter of 2006 meant England had held them for the shortest ever time, **462 days**.

The first mobile phone cost £2,000 and was the size of a briefcase.

A car salesman who thought he'd won the lottery told his boss to stick his job only to discover he had the wrong lottery numbers. *Muppet.*

The first words on MTV were: "*Ladies and gentlemen, rock and roll.*"

The human heart creates enough pressure when it pumps around the body to squirt blood thirty feet.

Judo comes from the Japanese words ju (gentle) and do (way) and was founded by Dr Jigoro Kano.

Aussie film star **Nicole Kidman** was nicknamed "**Stalky**" whilst at school because she was so tall and slim.

Little Britain star **David Walliams** used to be vegetarian, but he gave it up when he couldn't resist parma ham…

Steven Gerrard is the only footballer to have scored in the finals of the FA Cup, League Cup, Champions League and Uefa Cup.

Celebrity Big Brother's **Jermaine Jackson** married his brother Randy Jackson's ex wife Alejandra Genevieve Oaziaza.

Robbie Williams has a cat named Our Lady Kid. *It's the most tattooed cat in Los Angeles.*

Scarlett Johansson, Ashton Kutcher and **Simon Cowell** all have twin brothers.

Magician **Paul Daniels** has the personalised registration number **MAG1C**.

Movie actress **Angelina Jolie** had a childhood dream of becoming a funeral director.

Singing god **Justin Timberlake** played a young Elton John in the video for Elton's single "This Train Don't Stop There Any More".

Singing chef **Delia Smith**, Radio 2's gardener **Alan Titchmarsh**, *The Apprentice's* **Sir Alan Sugar** and PR guru **Max Clifford** all failed their 11-Plus, it's said.

Top chef **Jamie Oliver** became the first man in almost 70 years to be pictured on the cover of *Good Housekeeping*. He appeared in the magazine promoting his campaign to encourage families to eat together and was the first man on the cover since George VI in 1937.

Movie starlet **Lindsay Lohan** is allergic to blueberries.

The number of parking tickets issued to
motorists in the UK has quadrupled in the last
five years to more than three million.

The chances of having a **heart attack** during sex are
virtually nil, say scientists. Sudden and severe stress or
physical exertion is more likely to cause one. *What is sex if it's
not physical exertion?*

Top author Agatha Christie acquired her *knowledge of
poisons* while working in a hospital pharmacy during
World War One.

The distance between the government and opposition sides of the House of Commons is **two swords' lengths**.

The best busking pitch in any town is reckoned to be outside Marks and Spencer. *You can make a few bob and change your underwear at the same time. And perhaps meet Twiggy. And Myleene.*

Six endings were shot for the TV show **Cold Feet**, killing each of the six main characters, so no one would know who died until the episode went out. It was Rachel.

Exercising a dog is not only good for you but it wards off depression and loneliness, said a survey at the University of Portsmouth. *Nobody thought to ask the dog how he felt.*

The @ key on a computer keyboard is called a **strudel** in Israel, an **elephant's trunk** in Denmark and a **pickled herring** in Slovakia. *Do you believe that?*

Chanel No. 5 **perfume was the first ever advert on Channel 5.**

Eddie Knorn has installed a **58-foot railway carriage** in his front garden so motorists slow down to take a better look. *Although some mornings it doesn't arrive, or it's full, with standing room only.*

The things they say: "I couldn't settle in Italy – it was like living in a foreign country." Footballer Ian Rush on his time at Juventus.

Junk mail tops the poll of what we hate most about the postal service, beating post office closures, missing mail and long queues at the counter.

The average person in the UK will drink **80,000 cups of tea** during their life… *Not all at once. That would be very stressful for the bladder, rhymes with ladder.*

The Duke of Edinburgh **claimed he was the "world's second most experienced plaque unveiler"** when he stood in for the Queen on a visit to Arsenal's new football ground.

Robert De Niro worked several 12-hour shifts as a New York taxi driver in preparation for starring in *Taxi Driver*. *"You talking to me?"*

There are **6.2 million** dog owners in the UK.

Pupils at a school in Cornwall were ordered to cut down on the time they spent **hugging** because it was making them late for lessons and it was embarrassing for youngsters who didn't want to be hugged.

More and more of us are keeping exotic wildlife as pets. **12 lions, 14 tigers** and **50 leopards** are being kept as pets in the UK at present. *Crikey. Keep them on the lead.*

The average couple gets engaged 2 years, 11 months and 8 days after first meeting, according to 2008 research. **Somebody asked if I believe in sex before marriage. I said not if it makes you late for the ceremony.**

A Hebridean thrush flew **3,000 miles** to nest in a Canadian garden but experts said it was doomed after going all that way because there was no hope of finding a mate.

The first ever film score was by Saint-Saens (he composed "Carnival Of The Animals") for the 1908 film *L'Assassinat du Duc de Guise. He's the guy who did the one that goes "pom pom pom pom pom"...*

Footballer **Owen Hargreaves** was the only English player to score his penalty in the World Cup quarter-final shoot-out against Portugal in 2006. *It may have had something to do with him playing for a German league club at the time...*

About 15 million iPods are sold each Christmas yet sadly it's also your most likely piece of gadgetry to be stolen.

The **Arschleder** (arseleather) backside-sliding world championships are held annually in Germany. Contenders slide down a hill on bottoms protected only by leather breeches... Don't think any comic remarks are needed. Just close your eyes and picture them.

Film legend Sir Richard Attenborough says the reason he calls everyone **"darling"** and **"luvvie"** is nothing to do with passionately adoring them; he is just dreadful at remembering names.

One of the last things **Margaret Thatcher** did as Prime Minister was recommend the thesp Sir Ian McKellen for a knighthood.

Director Michael Winner always edits his films under the name of "Arnold Crust". *Calm down dear!*

Acting legend **Elizabeth Taylor** once topped a poll for Most Memorable Eyebrows. Lassie came second.

The actress **Jane Seymour** has one **brown** eye and one **green** eye. *Henry the Eighth still married her though, didn't he?*

Top luvvie **Helena Bonham Carter** is the great-granddaughter of former Prime Minister Lord Herbert Asquith.

Actress **Emma Thompson** is the sister of *EastEnders* star **Sophie Thompson** – Phil Mitchell's evil girlfriend, Stella, last seen spread-eagled over the bonnet of a car.

Despite his pronounced tones, luvvie **Kenneth Branagh** actually hails from a working-class area of Belfast.

Haaallllooooo ... actor **Leslie Phillips** went to elocution lessons as a child to get rid of his strong cockney accent. *Ding dong.*

At the premiere of the movie *The Queen* at the Venice Film Festival, **Helen Mirren** received a five-minute standing ovation.

Dame Judi Dench's Oscar™–winning performance as Queen Elizabeth I in the movie *Shakespeare in Love* lasted just 8 minutes.

Velvet-voiced thesp **Stephen Fry** spent several months in prison for credit card fraud when he was 18. He was caught after a hotel receptionist in Swindon became suspicious of him – she had questioned why a boy who wore shabby shoes would be in possession of two credit cards.

Before actor **Roger Moore** was cast as James Bond in *Live and Let Die*, Robert Redford, Paul Newman and Burt Reynolds were all considered for the part.

The UK's favourite actor **David Jason** won awards for his gymnastic skills whilst at school. *He who dares wins, Rodney.*

The actor **Simon Callow's** first job in theatre was in the Old Vic box office. He took it on the advice of acting giant Sir Laurence Olivier, who told him that if he was interested in acting, that was the place to start.

Sir Laurence Olivier himself is only the second actor to be buried in Poets' Corner in Westminster Abbey. The first was David Garrick.

Comic Relief Does The Apprentice drop-out **Rupert Everett** was in Moscow during the fall of communism, plus he was in Berlin the night the wall came down.

Thespian **Vanessa Redgrave** is the only person in Oscar™ history to win a Best Supporting Actress gong for playing the title role in a film. The film was *Julia*.

A credit card was issued to a cat called Messiah after its owner decided to test a bank's identity security system in Australia. *Messiah's now gone on to buy two cars and get a second mortgage on his flat.*

The number of miles we **drive** each year is falling for the first time since 1949. Higher road taxes and fuel costs are blamed. *Nothing to do with the traffic jams then.*

All one million **£5 notes** issued as a tribute to mark the first anniversary of **George Best's death** were sold within hours of their release.

Big Ben was named Britain's favourite landmark in a recent survey, with Stonehenge second. *My favourite landmark is Micky's Fish Bar in Paddington. Fish and chips 18 hours a day,* mmmmmmmmmmmmmmm.

The real first name of actress Sigourney Weaver is Susan.

Bath was the seventh most attractive place in a poll of World Heritage Sites, with The Great Wall of China and the Pyramids beaten to number one by Norway's fjords.

A prisoner in Austria wrapped himself in a parcel and **posted himself to freedom**. He unwrapped the parcel when clear of the prison and jumped off the back of a truck. The bubblewrap broke his fall.

Hollywood's greatest male star according to an American Film Institute poll was Humphrey Bogart. *Poll it again, Sam. If he can stand it, I can.*

We all sing it at the end of New Year's Eve but a survey shows only six per cent of us know the actual words to "Auld Lang Syne".

A man from Maldon in Essex became the first person in Britain to gain a darts PhD. His 200,000-word thesis was called "Darts in England 1900–1939 – A Social History". *Great, smashing, super.*

The only European countries where football isn't the most **popular spectator sport** are Ireland (Gaelic football), Finland (ice hockey) and Latvia and Estonia (basketball). *France (sex).*

John F Kennedy was not only the first Roman Catholic president of the United States, he was also the youngest ever.

Elephants can recognise their own reflection, placing them in an elite group of self-aware animals that includes humans, great apes and dolphins. *The trunk's a dead giveaway.*

Sitting at a computer screen all day is far more likely to cause us backache than manual work would. Lifting and carrying are dangerous but sitting still can be far worse.

Our food is now so full of preservatives that it will take our **corpses** three weeks to rot when once it took three days.

The mobile telephone number 666-6666 raised £1.4 million at an auction in Qatar.

Every time we take a step we move 54 muscles. How's that for keeping fit?

Sugababe **Keisha Buchanan** is the cousin of former Blue star Simon Webbe.

Celebrity Big Brother winner **Shilpa Shetty** is a black belt karate champion.

When **Kylie Minogue** first travelled to London to work with music producers Stock, Aitken and Waterman, they didn't know who she was and had forgotten that she was arriving. As a result, they wrote "I Should be So Lucky" while she waited outside the studio.

David Beckham wears a new pair of football boots for every game he plays, at an estimated cost of £300 a pair.

And **Victoria Beckham** is the only member of the Spice Girls not to have had a number one single as a solo artist.

Celebrity Big Brother star and glamour model **Danielle Lloyd** has claimed to have an IQ score of 152, making her eligible for Mensa membership.

Extras star and co-creator **Stephen Merchant** is 7ft 1in tall. And he has to put his head through a hole in the ceiling to present his radio show. But he's the cleverest and best-looking man in the city of Westminster, London. That's official.

Ricky Gervais can't drive.

Movie actress **Katie Holmes** auditioned for the role of Buffy Summers in *Buffy the Vampire Slayer*, but was turned down because she was too young. The role went to **Sarah Michelle Gellar**.

Celebrity section 6

A piece of amber with a spider trapped in it about 40 million years ago has been discovered in Rochester, Kent. The spider is a **dicranopalpus ramiger**... That's not what she said; she used a different adjective.

Billionaire Steve Wynn put his elbow through his **£80 million** Picasso painting. "Thank goodness it was me," he said.

More and more men are becoming house-husbands with a third of women now earning more than their male partners.

Cambridge and Oxford are the next **best universities** in the world, behind Harvard in the USA.

Asked to name a dying skill, four out of five people said good manners.
The other one said, "What's it to you?"

Whenever we start British Summer Time, clock collector Pauline West spends two days turning forward her 3,500 clocks. *What a waste of time.*

The deepest dive by an air-breathing animal is 6,230 foot (1,899 metres) by a **beaked whale**. It can hold its breath for 85 minutes while completing the dive.

Salman Rushdie, who became famous for his *Satanic Verses*, once told me that he is the man responsible for writing the advertising slogans "naughty but nice" and "irresistibubble" while working for the advertising industry in the 1970s.

Research at the University of Bath proved that **football referees** are more likely to penalise away teams than home ones in Premiership matches. *That was on the cards.*

Steve Wright

Organisers of the traditional World **Pie Eating** contest in Wigan were told to amend their competition from "who can eat the most meat and potato pies in three minutes" to "who can eat a single pie in the shortest time" to appease healthy-eating campaigners.

Only 13 per cent of us now go out on a Saturday night.

A **taxi driver** took two girls 90 miles out of their way when he keyed **Limington** in Somerset instead of **Lymington** in Hampshire into his sat-nav.

Pigeons can memorise more than 1,000 images for more than a year, say scientists at the Mediterranean Institute of Cognitive Neuroscience in Marseille. *So what? They still crap on your head.*

Hens lay more eggs when Radio 2 is played to them. *Especially my programme.*

There was no Miss Moneypenny in the 2006 version of Casino Royale.

Digital road signs informing motorists of the number of parking spaces in Crawley, Sussex, displayed obscene messages after hackers breached the council's computer server firewall.

A record number of Brits now work beyond the **official retirement age** – one in ten are still at work over 65 and one in nine women beyond 60.

The most played record of the last 70 years is **"A Whiter Shade of Pale"**, by Procol Harum. *They'll need to get a new one then.*

You can make **20 cans** out of recycled material with the same amount of energy it takes to make one new one.

The UK produces **420 million tonnes** of solid waste every year. That's the weight of 5 cars for each person every year. We only recycle 11 per cent of it.

Incinerating **10,000 tonnes** of waste creates 1 job, landfilling the same amount of waste creates 6 jobs, but recycling the same 10,000 tonnes creates 36 jobs.

In just over a week, we produce enough rubbish to fill the new **Wembley stadium**. Over half of that waste can be recycled.

Every tonne of paper recycled saves 17 trees.

Every year in the UK we use **13 billion steel cans** – if you placed them end to end, they would stretch to the moon… three times!

The energy saved from recycling one glass bottle is enough to power a light bulb for four hours.

Recycling one plastic bottle can save the same amount of energy needed to power a **60-watt light bulb** for six hours.

We use over **six billion glass bottles** and jars each year. It would take you over three and a half thousand years to sing "Six Billion Green Bottles"!

Only **1 per cent** of the world's water supply is usable; 97 per cent is in the ocean and 2 per cent is frozen.

The **salmon** was named as the symbol that best represents the British environment, according to a poll of staff at the Environment Agency. *It whiffs a bit.*

Fans of tennis star Andy Murray got to choose his new hairstyle by voting on his website.

Puppies replaced children in the Andrex ads on the advice of advertising regulators.

An advert for **Smash** instant mashed potato was voted the best TV food commercial of all time. *You know, the ones with the tin aliens that laugh.*

Gerrards Cross in Buckinghamshire is the most expensive place to buy a home in Britain, with **£725,000** being the average cost of a house.

We spend more on **wine** than any other European country. Even France, where wine is now seen as old-fashioned.

Sixty per cent of British **orchards** have been lost in the last 50 years, even though we're supposed to eat more fruit and veg.

Portsmouth have held the FA Cup for the longest continuous time. They won it in 1939 and kept it until 1946 because of the war.

Woad was once used as blue dye before being superseded by indigo. *That was the end of the woad.*

Aardvarks are only found in Africa. *...and at the start of alphabetical lists of animals.*

Britain's Association of Personal Assistants has been swamped with enquiries from people wanting careers – inspired by the TV show *Ugly Betty*.

A well-driven golf ball can reach speeds of up to 170mph.

Nobody knows what's what.

The nearest motorway to Lowestoft is  in Holland.

Soho in London is named after an ancient hunting cry. *Which goes like this...* "Where's Starbucks?"

The words of the Labour Party Anthem, "Red Flag", were written by Jim Connell on the top of a number 28 London bus when he was wound up after a political meeting.

"Garlic bread. It's the future, I've tasted it." Peter Kay had the "funniest one-liner in television history" according to a viewers' poll. **"So what first attracted you to the millionaire Paul Daniels?"** – Caroline Aherne, as Mrs Merton, interviewing Debbie McGee – came second.

Jemini were the first UK act to score nil points in the Eurovision Song Contest.

A banana is the most common pretend weapon for criminals, according to university researchers. *Hands up which student got a loan for 3 years to find that out?*

Actor **Robert Lindsay** ended up in hospital suffering from shock and had to have gravel picked out of his knees after coming off a scooter while filming TV show *Citizen Smith*.

We send an average of **37 texts** a month, compared to 21 five years ago. *I know people who send 37 texts a day!*

Blue cars are the most likely to break down, and drivers born under the star sign Libra are most likely to be driving them, say car insurers who, for some pointless reason, study this sort of thing!

Sylvia Miles had the shortest ever **Oscar**™**-nominated** performance. She appeared in *Midnight Cowboy* for six minutes.

A US airline has decided to sell advertising space on its air sickness bags. *That makes me want to throw up.*

Conkers can be stored behind heavy furnishings to deter moths. *But it's not compulsory.*

Naked Jungle, the Channel 5 game show in which presenter Keith Chegwin went nude, topped the list of worst television shows of all time. *Some viewers complained they needed a magnifying glass.*

Burnt Out But Opulent was abbreviated to Bobo in Yuppie-speak.

The Prime Minister has revealed his four-year-old son John can beat him at tennis on his Nintendo Wii games console.

"Above Us Only Sky", from **John Lennon's** "Imagine", can be seen on signs at Liverpool Airport (which is called John Lennon Airport).

Homer Simpson was recognised by more people in a survey than Britain's ex prime minister Tony Blair or Jesus Christ. *More than even Richard and Judy, you say? Surely not.*

Three Mexican fishermen drifted in the Pacific for 10 months after the engines on their boat failed. They lived on raw seagulls, fish and rainwater. *Then after that they ate the engine.*

Eight is the average age at which a child gets a mobile phone.

When film star **Tom Cruise** was younger, his sisters and their friends would put him on the kitchen sink and practise kissing him.

Actresses **Jennifer Ellison**, **Charlize Theron** and **Penelope Cruz** all trained as ballet dancers.

I'm a Celebrity... star **Jason Donovan** is the half-brother of current *Neighbours* star **Stephanie McIntosh**, who plays Sky Mangel.

And **Jason** once sent in an audition tape of himself singing to TV show *Stars in Their Eyes*, but failed to even get an audition.

When movie actor **Jude Law** joined the National Youth Music Theatre, he was placed in the wrong dormitory because staff thought he was a girl because of his name. He never told anyone but was soon caught and moved.

TV's **Ant and Dec** are insured against each other's death.

Dancing on Ice star **Lisa Scott Lee** is a quarter Chinese through her grandfather.

TV presenter Richard Madeley presented the never transmitted pilot of *You've Been Framed*.

British model **Jordan's** bustline has grown, over her career, from 32B to 34G.

Presenter **Kate Thornton** is nicknamed "Philadelphia", because her high voice is said to be similar to that of the actress who starred in the adverts for the soft cheese.

A British three-year-old called Jack bought a £9,000 shocking pink Barbie Nissan Figaro car on e-Bay by fiddling with his mum's computer.

Flamingos can live for up to 80 years. *That's not a flamingo dancer, they live in Spain.*

An **Irish billionaire** reportedly bid more than 2 million dollars at a charity auction to play a round of golf with Tiger Woods. He could have got Terry Wogan for much less.

Astronauts are expected to go to the moon in 2020 – for the first time since 1972. *You know what will happen – three rockets will come along at once. And when they get there, as usual – absolutely no atmosphere.*

A new breed of dog was shown at Crufts this year. It was a small, spaniel-type dog called a kooikerhondje – *but you can call it* **Buster.**

The London Borough of Hackney banned the use of the word manholes as it's sexist and "an insult to women". *I dread to think what the alternative might be.*

A large swarm of locusts can eat **80,000 tonnes** of corn a day. *Why would they want to do that?*

Humans get a buzz from **crunching** into crisps or biscuits, say experts, the ultrasound waves for each bite making for a more pleasurable eating experience. *I don't like it when a tooth snaps off though, or when I end up eating a pencil. I don't like that, I don't like that.*

Ex-champion jockey **Frankie Dettori** has a line of pizzas and ice creams and owns a string of restaurants. But his own diet consists of three peas a day to keep his weight down. *Frankie, that's hardly substantial.*

"He Ain't Heavy, He's My Brother" was a hit for **The Hollies** in 1969 but took until 1988 to reach number one.

Da Vinci wrote backwards to stop smudges. *I said… sdrawkcab etorw icniV aD.*

Tourists still ask for directions to the house in **Notting Hill** where the Hugh Grant–Julia Roberts movie was filmed – even though the famous blue door has been **auctioned off** and replaced by one of a different colour.

Bats always turn left when exiting a cave. *I do the same out of my garage.*

An **Indian farmer** said he would try for more children after becoming a dad at the age of 88. He puts his sexual longevity down to long walks and drinking camel's milk.

When **Chris Kirkland** made his England football debut, his dad won nearly £10,000 after getting odds of 100–1 ten years earlier that Chris would play for his country one day.

Ex-Pulp frontman Jarvis Cocker impersonated Rolf Harris to win *Celebrity Stars In Their Eyes*. Did you know who he was yet?

The rain lashing down during her weather bulletin on Central TV prompted a confused forecaster to reveal it was "pissing down". Two viewers complained.

Millions of trees are planted by forgetful squirrels.

When she was in her teens, Fiona Bruce appeared in a number of romantic photo-stories for *Jackie* magazine.

Channel 4 newsreader Jon **Snow** and former *Newsnight* presenter Peter Snow are cousins.

And Jon Snow declined an OBE in **2000**, and later made a documentary entitled "Secrets of the Honours System".

BBC Breakfast's Bill Turnbull owns *four* hives of bees.

Staying with bees, **BBC One** newsreader Sophie Raworth made her first TV appearance aged fourteen when she appeared in a BBC report for *Nationwide* about her mother's bee-keeping enterprise.

BBC newsreader Kenneth Kendall once lost a tooth in the middle of a live broadcast. The **false crown** fell out of his mouth and landed on his desk.

Natasha Kaplinsky was once **voted** "Most Ageing Hairstyle" in a women's magazine.

Anna Ford and Reginald Bosanquet used to play darts in the production office before going on air to read the news at ITN.

And Anna Ford was told she was too old to become a newsreader when she joined Granada Television as a researcher, aged 30, in **1974**. She read her last news bulletin for the BBC in 2006, aged 62.

Peter Sissons went to **junior school** with John Lennon and funnyman Jimmy Tarbuck.

Newsnight's Jeremy Paxman became the focus of media attention himself in **2000** when the stolen Enigma machine which had been taken from Bletchley Park Museum was inexplicably sent to him in the post. He returned it.

Angela Rippon once had a top ten album, Shape up and Dance with Angela Rippon.

Five's Kirsty Young used to go out with presenter and **computer whizz** Dominik Diamond.

The late Reginald Bosanquet was said to wear a hairpiece because he had to shave off some of his hair occasionally, the result of the condition dermatitis.

BBC presenter Emily Maitliss is fluent in Mandarin.

Richard Baker was the first television newsreader. His voice was heard on bulletins from 1954. However Kenneth Kendall was the first television newsreader to be actually seen, in **1955**.

Gloria Gaynor's feminist anthem
"I Will Survive" was intended
as a B-side.

Gold cost more in 1980 – £460 an ounce – than it does now.

A car licence plate bearing just the number **1** fetched
£7 million at a charity auction in Abu Dhabi.

A satellite-tracking device on the back of
a leatherback turtle recorded it covered at
least 13,000 miles in the Pacific – and then the
tag's power supply ran out. By the time the
repair guy got there the turtle was dead.
"I thought you said 11 o'clock?"
Sorry mate, we can't specify a time.

Next to man (and woman) the **porpoise**
is the most intelligent creature on earth.
That's because it's the only creature
with a true sense of porpoise.

Rotund comedian Johnny Vegas studied ceramics at Middlesex University.

Slimming club **Weight Watchers** was founded in the early 1960s by a New Yorker who invited friends to her home for coffee and asked if they would join her on a diet.

The number of people admitted to hospital with **bee, wasp** or **hornet** stings has more than doubled to 843 in a year. Actual deaths from stings total about eight a year.

More than 150 people presented *Top of The Pops* in 2,204 editions before it folded. Among the best known were Sir Jimmy Saville, Tony Blackburn, Mike Read, Janice Long and Edith Bowman. *Oh and who was that good-looking one? I know ... Steve Wright! (Geeky thin bloke.)*

Escapologist Karl Bartoni and his fiancée were married in 1984 while suspended from Blackpool Tower in a cage.

Croatia has more than 1,000 islands. *Over here we put them on our salad.*

Left-handed university graduates earn an average of 21 per cent more than right-handed ones, says research.

Mickey Mouse was the first non-human to win an Oscar™.

Camels have three eyelids to protect their eyes from blowing sand. *That sounds like an odd habit.*

Candy floss was invented in America in 1897 and was originally called fairy floss.

Flip-flops are called jandals in New Zealand and thongs in Australia. "Pass my thongs, darling, I'm going out to light the Barbie."

We Brits now spend more eating out than in, up to £85 billion a year.

Vic Reeves' real name of Jim Moir is the same as his father and grandfather. All three share the same birthday. *January 24th, since you ask.*

A monkey called Betty who escaped from London Zoo last year returned of her own accord after more than 12 hours roaming treetops in Regent's Park.

The human heart pumps between 1,350 and 1,650 gallons of blood in a day.

How do we cope with **stress?** According to a survey, Italians brawl and bonk, the French take a long soak in the bath, Americans turn to food and Brits to alcohol.

People who make "ugly faces" at dogs in Oklahoma can be jailed.

Henry I of England sired more than 25 children, only two of them illegitimate. He was also known as Henry Beauclerc, because of his scholarly interests. *He must have put those books down sometimes, though.*

Sgt Pepper's Lonely Hearts Club Band has been voted the nation's favourite number one album. *Thriller*, by Michael Jackson, was second. *Floral Dance, the album by Terry Wogan, third.*

The amount of sturgeon caught annually has gone from
35,000 tonnes a year a century ago to 1,000 tonnes now.
Most are caught in the Caspian.
That's very painful.

A charity game of **conger cuddling**, played between teams in Lyme Regis who try to knock each other off wooden blocks with a dead conger, has been banned after an anonymous animal-rights protest.

Robert De Niro copied gangster Al Capone by wearing silk underwear to play him in *The Untouchables*, even though his skimpies were never seen on screen.

Furniture company MFI was founded in 1964 as Mullard Furniture Industries.

A restaurant called **The Reindeer** opened for just the month of December in London, with the slogan: *"The Reindeer is not for life, it's just for Christmas."*

Pop star **Emma Bunton** is the great-great-great-great-great-great-grandniece of **Archduke William Pinkley-Hogue of Staffordshire**, making her 103rd in line for the throne of England. *Queen Baby Spice the 1st.*

Music star **Myleene Klass** comes from six generations of classical musicians on her father's side. She herself began to learn the piano and violin from the age of 4 and the harp at 12.

An anagram of **Gordon Ramsay** is "So angry or mad".

Top Gear star **Jeremy Clarkson's** mother made her fortune selling Paddington Bear merchandise.

007 star **Daniel Craig** is the first Bond actor to have been born *after* the Bond series began.

And Craig's middle name is **Wroughton**.

When they began filming the hit TV show *Life on Mars*, actors **John Simm** and **Philip Glenister** decided to wear Old Spice and Brut to try and get the Seventies smell every morning. They did it once, but smelt so much they didn't do it again...

And **John Simm** features on an album by Echo and the Bunnymen singer Ian McCulloch, singing backing vocals.

Before turning to television presenting, TV presenter **Davina McCall** tried to make it as a singer. Her demo disc was produced by Eric Clapton.

Dancing on Ice champion **Kieran Bracken** had his two front teeth knocked out and embedded in a fellow player's head during a match in 1992, but had to wait until he officially retired from the sport before he could have any permanent repairs done.

Grease is the Word judge **Sinitta** apparently had a two-year relationship with **Brad Pitt** during the 1980s.

X Factor winner **Leona Lewis** wrote her first song at the age of 12.

And **Lewis** made music history when her debut single was downloaded **50,000 times in just 30 minutes**.

Girls Aloud star **Sarah Harding** once entered lads mag *FHM's* national beauty contest – High Street Honeys – and her pictures appeared in the first Top 100. She later withdrew from the competition after achieving success on the TV show, *Popstars*. Just one year later, however, she was voted one of the Top 30 sexiest women in the world by readers of the same magazine.

The producers of *Big Brother* gave **Marcus Bentley** the job of narrator because they liked the way he said "chickens".

TV presenter **Zoe Ball** was called "FA Cup" when she was at school because of the shape of her ears.

Before becoming famous as one third of Atomic Kitten, **Kerry Katona** performed on stage as a lap dancer.

The **oldest president** in the USA was Ronald Reagan. He was 77 in 1988.

The record for running the 1,576 steps to the observation deck on the 86th floor of the Empire State building is 9 minutes 33 seconds.

Studies at Polytechnic University in New York revealed that commuting to work is stressful and that the longer the journey the more stressful it can be. *Next year they're investigating whether swimming makes you wet.*

The movie *Patton* won the Oscar™ for **best film** in 1971, the year of release for controversial British film *Clockwork Orange. Rhymes with… what does Orange rhyme with? P.S. The greatest factoid in history is… that nothing rhymes with orange. Apart from another orange.*

A foreign driver is let off a speeding ticket every six minutes because it's not worth the authorities doing the paperwork. He's a very lucky boy, then!

A **seaweed** used to flavour Japanese food, called Undaria Pinnatifida, has been shown to cause weight loss in animals, particularly around the abdomen, and might be developed into a slimming supplement. *So if you're a hippo, look out for the "Undaria Pinnatifida Weight Loss Programme", coming soon to a cable channel near you.*

A **retired surgeon** became the oldest man to swim the Channel in 2006, 65-year-old Roger Allsop completing the crossing in just over 15 hours despite suffering seasickness. *Luckily he had a brown bag and a boiled sweet in his trunks.*

Speedway riders race at up to 80mph despite having no brakes on their bikes.

All but three minutes of the movie *12 Angry Men* took place in the jury room. *Wonder how much the set designer got on that gig.*

Italians play a version of the game of boules or petanque and call it bocce. *Bocce lot of people know that.*

The UK has bigger primary-school classes than almost any other industrialised nation, with an average of 26 pupils in each class.

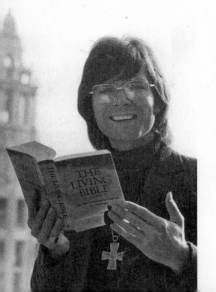

The happiest and most self-fulfilled celebrity according to a nationwide survey is **Cliff Richard(s)**. He was just ahead of the Dalai Lama and the Togmeister. *You don't often get those two in the same sentence… We don't think the Dalai Lama has ever done Pause for Thought.*

Global warming is blamed for a drastic shrinking of the Arctic ice cap, with an area the size of Turkey disappearing in a year. *Don't suppose it actually was Turkey by any chance?*

One in ten of our **horse chestnut trees** is infected with disease. *A right old conker canker.*

Cauliflowers can now be grown in orange, purple and green to bring a **splash of colour** to your dinner table.

The French oral (if you'll pardon the expression) has been scrapped from **GCSE** exams, because the stress of speaking French stops kids from choosing to study it.

The trendy Conservative **torch emblem** in the form of a scribbled oak tree was described by Lord Tebbit as looking like a bunch of broccoli. *Mind you, so were the Cabinet that year.*

Plumbers, tilers and plasterers are being sought by Australia to fill a skills gap.

More than 2.6 million people in the UK officially suffer from asthma.

One in two teenagers is in the red before they reach 17, admitting they see **credit cards** as an easy way to spend cash they haven't got.

The **motorcycle** Steve McQueen rode in *The Great Escape* was the same one Henry Winkler rode in *Happy Days*. *Strange, but I thought Steve McQueen wrecked it when he ploughed it into that steel fence.*

A couple who met at the **Tall Persons Club** of Great Britain have the combined height of 13ft 7in – he's 7ft 4in and she's 6ft 3in. *Love was in the air when they met.*

Youngsters who do not get enough sleep are more likely to become overweight.

A rare edition of **Geoffrey Chaucer's** works that was found beneath a pile of pullovers in a wardrobe (in Streatham) fetched £74,000 at auction.

Fitness, say experts, can be achieved by a few minutes of full-out exercise a day – such as **high-intensity cycling** – relieving us all of the excuse that we haven't got time to exercise.

Long-running soap *Coronation Street* was originally intended to run for 13 episodes. *Now it's coming up to its 257 millionth episode.*

During the first five days of the hit show *24*, counter-terrorist agent Jack Bauer killed 114 people.

Harrods began as a grocer's shop near Colchester in Essex, founded by Charles Henry Harrod (1799–1885).

The album *Abbey Road* was going to be called **"Everest"**.

The Beatles' first album, *Please Please Me*, was recorded in **just one day**.

Ringo Starr is left handed but has always played a right-handed drum kit.

Paul McCartney wrote "When I'm 64" for his dad Jim on his 64th birthday.

When **Ringo Starr** first replaced Pete Best permanently at a Cavern Club show, George Harrison got a black eye from an angry Pete Best fan.

In a contest held by **Merseyside Newspaper** to see who was the biggest band in Liverpool in 1962, one of the main reasons that The Beatles won was because they called in posing as different people voting for themselves, allegedly.

One of **John Lennon's** school reports read "Certainly on the road to failure."

"Help!" was the first Beatles song not to be about **love**.

Ringo Starr was the first Beatle to return from the band's visit to India in the spring of 1968, to study with Maharishi Mahesh Yogi. Despite packing cans of baked beans, he didn't like the spicy food in camp.

The Beatles became **millionaires in 1965**.

Ringo Starr, **Paul McCartney** (and his then wife **Linda**), and **George Harrison** have all guest starred on *The Simpsons*, although not at the same time.

It was Decca A&R man **Dick Rowe** who **rejected The Beatles** early in 1962, choosing instead to sign Brian Poole and the Tremeloes.

"Strawberry Fields Forever" was actually two versions of the song mixed together by **George Martin**. One was half a tone higher and slightly faster. The Beatles liked both versions and couldn't decide on one and asked Martin if he could put them together somehow.

Before he produced The Beatles,
George Martin worked on comedy albums.

The Beatles and **The Rolling Stones** used to agree not to release their singles and albums at the same time, to allow each the chance to reach number one in the charts.

A Hard Day's Night was the first Beatles album to consist entirely of *songs they had written themselves*.

A typical live Beatles show lasted just **35 minutes**, because the boys couldn't hear themselves sing, owing to the **screaming**.

The Beatles recorded versions of "I Want to Hold Your Hand" and "She Loves You" **in German**. Neither translated well and they vowed **never to do it again**.

The things they say: *"We didn't underestimate them. They were just better than we thought."* Manager Bobby Robson after an England game.

Scientists working on a cure for **baldness** reckon they will have perfected a technique involving injections by the end of the decade.

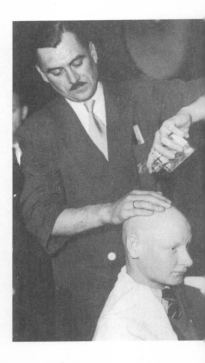

The artist JMW Turner asked sailors to lash him to a mast so he could experience a storm at sea. *Turner was later in the Solvite advert. See his exhibition The Solvite Years at the National Gallery soon.*

Osama Bin Laden **shares the same birthday with** Mark Chapman, **who shot John Lennon, and** James Earl Ray, **who murdered Martin Luther King.**

Music lessons improve **memory** and **IQ** and could be one of the best things for a child's education, say researchers.

Residents of **Bournemouth** are the happiest in the UK according to a survey, with 82 per cent saying they were happy because of lovely beaches, a bustling town centre, nice gardens and good sports facilities...

Walsall came out worst with 46 per cent. *It sure could do with a beach, Walsall*.

The image we all have of Cleopatra as a seductive beauty has been ruined by the unearthing of an ancient coin which showed her with a shallow forehead, pointed chin, thin lips and a hooked nose. *They said she looked like Keith Richards' granddad*.

A standard golf ball has **336 dimples**. *Des O'Connor has only one.*

Melvyn Bragg's *South Bank Show* is the third-longest running TV programme, after *Coronation Street* and *Emmerdale*.

The first opera was *Dafne*, written around 1597 by Jacopo Peri.

English teenagers learn the fewest languages in Europe, says an EU report, 0.6 against an average of 1.4 in the other member states.

The Gaelic words on the headstone of **Spike Milligan** read: Duirt me leat go raibh me breoite (I told you I was ill).

Guests went home with a £15,000 goodie bag containing boots, perfume, truffles, cosmetics and a game console from the 2007 Brit Awards.

A 12-step recovery programme has been drawn up for email addicts. *This is the modern world.*

The over-50s are responsible for more carbon emissions than any other age group, because of high car use, holidays abroad and eating out.

If you want to become a dad, take **showers instead of hot baths** as scientists have confirmed the old wives' tale that prolonged immersion in hot water decreases male fertility.

A wine taster in Holland has insured his nose for **5 million euros** to make sure he would be compensated if he couldn't ever smell the vino.

Thirty people have drowned trying to attempt the same canoe journey as in the film *Deliverance*.

If you press firmly when **spreading butter** on your toast it's more likely to fall butter side up if you drop it, because the knife creates a convex indentation. *Oh! That's why, then!*

Elizabeth Taylor did all her own riding, including stunts, in the film *National Velvet*.

Sixty-five per cent of children don't know how to **boil an egg**, with millions of parents not passing on even the simplest of cooking skills they were taught as youngsters.

A cup of **cocoa** could increase your brain power and may even help treat dementia, because the natural nutrients increase blood flow to the brain.

A snowboarder stranded at night 5,000ft up a mountain in the French Alps was saved after flashing the light from his mobile phone at a rescue helicopter. *Do you know, I research them and write them but some of them I just don't believe…*

Bloodhounds are on the way to
extinction after total annual births
in Britain fell to just 70.

The first names of **Mr Humphries**, as played by the late
great John Inman in *Are You Being Served?*, were Wilberforce
Clayborne.

**Older men who
drink** moderate
amounts of
alcohol **are
better at
routine tasks
such as** walking
and climbing
**than
teetotallers,
scientists have
discovered**.

Actor **Ewan McGregor** is an accomplished French horn player.

In 2003, TV presenter **Claudia Winkleman** raised money for Comic Relief by getting people to sponsor her for every hour she was in labour with her first child, who was due on Red Nose Day. It lasted 23 hours.

TV presenter **Tess Daly** was born Helen Elizabeth Tess Daly.

Strictly Come Dancing **Bruce Forsyth's** catchphrases are so well known that some of them feature in the *Oxford Dictionary of Quotations*. *Didn't he do well?*

Sir Andrew Lloyd Webber and **Steve Redgrave** are both diabetic.

Cat Deeley owns the last former home of Marilyn Monroe, in which Marilyn was found dead.

Fame Academy presenter **Patrick Kielty** hosted the original pilot of the American version of *Deal or No Deal* for the ABC network in early 2004. However, ABC decided against airing the series, which ended up on rival network NBC with Canadian comedian Howie Mandal as host.

Singer **Beyoncé Knowles** has admitted that in order to get over her natural shyness she developed a stage persona named "Sasha".

Location Location Location presenter **Kirstie Allsopp** is the daughter of the 6th Baron Hindlip and is entitled to be referred to as The Honourable Kirstie Allsopp.

Strictly Come Dancing judge **Len Goodman** got into dancing after he hurt his foot playing football. His doctor said that his bones would never heal well enough for him to make it as a professional footballer and suggested swimming or ballroom dancing instead. Len didn't know where his nearest swimming pool was so his girlfriend booked him ballroom dancing lessons.

"Restaurant" is the most misspelled word in internet search engines.

Were you aware that **one fifth** of everyone living in Britain will eat a curry this weekend?

In the original **Monopoly**, tactically the best properties to buy are the orange ones: Vine Street, Marlborough Street and Bow Street.

Of the **147 million** Americans on the Internet, 12 million have blogs...*8 million of them thought a blog was some kind of varicose vein.*

The word "clock" comes from the **Latin word** "clocca", which means bell.

We accumulate more than a ton of unwanted clothes in our lifetime, which we'll never wear. *Although Russell Brand wears them anyway. (We only mention Russell Brand so that we can mention him. No offence, Russ.)*

Super nurse **Florence Nightingale** always travelled with her pet owl in her pocket. *Not very hygienic.*

Amanda Holden's first TV appearance was as a contestant on *Blind Date*. **She wasn't picked.**

Three-quarters of us now work in **service** industries such as property sales, finance and leisure, rather than manufacturing, as in the past.

Madonna named her daughter Lourdes as a tribute to her mother, who wanted to visit Lourdes in France, but died before doing so.

Buster Keaton starred in more than 100 films. *Think of all those lines he had to learn.*

Crystal Palace is the only Football League team whose name starts with five consonants. *Thank you, Carol. Back to you, Des. P.S. Des, you may be eating too many oranges.*

Dave Cornthwaite skateboarded 3,638 miles across Australia, covering 38 miles a day, for charity.

Footballer's wife **Cheryl Cole** was the first person to be voted into Girls Aloud on the TV show *Pop Stars: The Rivals.*

German women due to give birth at the end of last year tried to delay the moment until 2007 to cash in on generous family subsidies.

The world's tallest building at the end of the 19th century was the Eiffel Tower.

The film *The Color Purple* received 11 Oscar™ nominations but didn't win any.

A breakfast of toast and honey is the ideal New Year's Day hangover cure, according to the Royal Society of Chemistry. *And Doctor Hilary Jones.*

Former Prime Ministers **Tony Blair** and **Baroness Thatcher**, plus **Bob Mortimer**, **Fidel Castro** (*not Fidel Castrol GTX, that's an oil*) and the late TV presenter **Sir Robin Day** all qualified as lawyers.

Tennis star **Monica Seles'** name is an anagram of "camel noises". *Which is just the kind of noise she makes when lobbing.*

Gruff-voiced actor **Ray Winstone** had 88 amateur boxing bouts as a youngster and twice represented England. *Don't look at me, I ain't gonna tell you what to do.*

Madonna, **Keira Knightley** and **Uma Thurman** are all keen fencers. *Not of stolen goods. Actual sword fighting.*

Actor **Patrick Troughton** is reputed to have given up the role of Doctor Who in 1969 because he felt the series had been done to death and wouldn't last.

Top actor **Christian Slater** made an uncredited appearance in the film *Austin Powers: International Man of Mystery* as a security guard.

Strictly Come Dancing champion and cricketer **Darren Gough** was born on the day Jimi Hendrix died – 18/09/70.

Movie legend **Clint Eastwood** wore the same boots in TV series *Rawhide* as for the Western film *Unforgiven* more than 30 years later.

British soul star **Lemar** only came third in BBC's *Fame Academy* in 2002. He was beaten by **David Sneddon** and **Sinead Quinn**.

Women were found to get a better deal than men when buying a car, according to "secret shopper" research.

Scientists can now identify where you last drank water by analysing your hair. *Why would they want to do that? Do they all work for Evian?*

"**Chameleon**" sunglasses with lenses that change colour at the touch of a button have been developed by boffins in America.

The only country which is crossed by both the Equator and the Tropic of Capricorn is *Brazil.*

A wealthy businessman who found out he was dying before he could fulfil his plan to retire in Sidmouth, Devon, left the seaside town his £1.5 million fortune.

Davide Dennis survived 12 days of getting lost in a **dense Italian forest** by living on chestnuts and rainwater. *Old chestnuts are always the best. That's a pun.*

A four-day food and wine festival in Birmingham turned dry when organisers forgot to apply for an alcohol licence.

A mobile phone carries more germs than a toilet seat. *I blame the eight-year-olds.*

Archbishop **Desmond Tutu** took his wife to Disneyland to celebrate their ruby wedding.

Former *X Factor* judge **Louis Walsh** has had a song named after him – "Louis Walsh" by Irish band The Revs.

DIY has never been less popular, says a recent survey, with the numbers who can put up shelves dropping from 65 to 55 per cent. *"We can't be bothered,"* was the main reason.

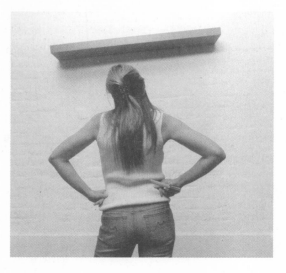

Noddy Holder has seen the film *Cabaret* about 100 times. *How many times did Liza Minnelli see Slade?*

A rare and protected species of seahorse has been found in the River Thames – it was hiding in the mud near Dagenham.

Remember – no matter how small a jockey you are, you just can't ride 'em!

Taking **afternoon naps** can dramatically cut the risk of heart disease.